Hour of the Green Light

❧

David Ruekberg

FUTURECYCLE PRESS
www.futurecycle.org

Cover artwork, "Pleiades Cluster [M45]" by NASA, JPL-Caltech, J. Stauffer; author photo by Tonya Kostenko; cover and interior book design by Diane Kistner; Adobe Garamond text and titling

Library of Congress Control Number: 2020947259

Published by FutureCycle Press
Athens, Georgia, USA

ISBN 978-1-952593-03-1

To my mother, Nancy, for flesh,
and my father, Benjamin, for spirit.

Rest in peace.

Contents

Delivery

Calendar

So

Night Walk

The Questions

Where I Came From

I talk to my inner lover, and I say, why such rush?
We sense that there is some sort of spirit that loves
     birds and animals and the ants—
perhaps the same one who gave a radiance to you
     in your mother's womb.
Is it logical you would be walking around entirely
     orphaned now?
The truth is you turned away yourself,
and decided to go into the dark alone.
Now you are tangled up in others, and have forgotten
     what you once knew,
and that's why everything you do has some weird
     failure in it.

—Kabir

Delivery

Delivery

Swimming away from the green horizon
I foresaw hot light and desiccation

sweetened by a swirl of apricot and apple
that would soon enough sour.

Birds stirred, fluttered my belly.
Scenting life, I gave way to gravity.

The amber world heaved in a way
that was terrible and fun.

I was too new to understand paradox—
the seasick fish, the cascade of sand.

Some tremendous force of love
pressed down on my sun-shaped face.

I came to know what the amputee knows,
leaving behind my perfect self forever.

What I didn't expect was the havoc,
the calipers tipped with fire,

the rigid god who hung me in air,
an aborted sacrifice.

The new world closed
its rubber hand around me

like a tourniquet, dandling me,
inverted and wrawling,

before the crowd, its roar
rasping my brand-new skin.

Embarkation

One dark enfolds and pours us
out of one ocean and into
a certain gravity.

The one we know in nightmares
and heart attack
is a falling only.

We wear the twilight
of this world, a conflagration
of mirrors in water and stone.

Yearning become a promise
of return. Our skin a ticket
with the entry burned in.

The Only Sure Thing

I couldn't see anything anyway
except the backs of people's heads

and the lights themselves.
But when the lights went out

I heard the hush that had fallen before.
And the cry of the many,

not of the one man who had fallen.
It was a rodeo. I was four.

The Bakers had taken me, friends
of our mother's in that tiny

Cumberland town, old poor folks
whose house smelled of coffee,

bacon, damp paper. Like American
Gothic, revised, they were.

He, timid, his bony angles little
defense. She, bossy with him,

but with us all the woman
you'd expect from one so round.

In our kitchen she nursed us
with oats and eggs, pressed me

to her bosom when my mother
would have scolded

the bloodied finger pinched
in the toy car's sharp hinge.

It wasn't my first taste of death—
the dust of the stadium

and the hushed exit, the dust
in the corners of their two rooms.

There was my birth, too, and the way
I waved goodbye to my first self

as the tunnel pressed me towards
a second shape, and the light burned.

Something was cut, but I didn't know it.
Something called me home, but I didn't hear.

I was in love with being held, and it was
a long time before I felt I was alone.

One evening I cried out in my crib.
By the time my mother took me up

I had discovered the emptiness
that we have made a god of.

What would we give for Mrs. Baker's
sour breast? What could we say

that would get her to turn to her cowering man
and forgive him his loneliness,

to swipe the dust from their shelves
and watch it buck the sunny air?

After Easter

The taste of Jesus
when I was five

was plastic and white
with a little gold paint.

The booklet of Beatitudes
so crinkled and waxy,

sky blue, warm peach
and creamy.

The music of Jesus
was sweet and sad.

The nails in his palms
like roses.

How I wished
I could join him

up there, so sweetly
suffering.

The rooms of my house
so square and solid.

The blue of the walls
dim in the corners.

Cicatrix

Leaves that should have fallen by now—
so late in the season—flutter and threaten

but hold. We spoke last night about betrayal,
secrets we were asked to keep,

a ghost in the room still holding us
without hands, braiding a cicatrix

between that chamber we've assigned to love
and sunlight—a knot made fast

by F-150s filling the rearview mirror
and domestic tanks renouncing sky and earth

to get to the game on time.
Does the fog of hurts suffered in the crib

and everything after also hang on faithful dogs
and birds too scared to come to the feeder,

or is this affliction purely human,
like math and conjugation?

Rain is forecast for tomorrow,
followed by terrific winds.

It's not practical to sit here with my pen,
pinned behind the picture window,

with so much to do to prepare for winter.
Tomorrow the leaves will surely all come down.

Happy Hour

Four o'clock. The sun's been sliding
all afternoon. Hour of my first expulsion.

Hour of the cherished time between school bus
and heated family dinners.

Hour of the relative sunshine of adolescence,
circles of friends, the ache for romance and sex

in that order. Then college—actual sex and romance
filled and emptied and filled again.

Hour of the long road of manhood muted
at day's end by glasses of wine or vodka and ice,

the first sips bringing a brightening—the lowering
grey of workplace humiliations and highway wrangles

lifting—as when a long coastal winter gives way
to a shift in currents, the socked-in cliffs'

shrouds ripped by a wedge of horizon.
Then the slit widens, becomes actual blue sky.

One more drink, and all is seen as in a glass
globe, plastic palm trees and bronzed girls

frozen in grass skirts littered with fake snow.
One more, and I crawl down the phantom

tunnel, not remembering, exactly—except
in the breadcrumb trail of amnesiac longing—

the bliss of the graveless grotto
to which I will never return.

Brief History

It's not that I got over my fear of death.
I just became too busy to remember.

So I avoided an intimacy with strangers,
which was all I really wanted.

I studied the plastic breastplate
and the plastic sword I'd begged for as a child,

made them stronger with a collection
of daily insults. The imagined ones were best.

I erased the memories of fear and pain,
then erased the erasures, bleached

the unsoiled linens, forgave the forgiven.
I skirted the camouflage of moss and sticks

I'd built above the vertiginous void
that was my hell and my salvation.

So I announced my arrival at an arctic bliss
in the order of my clips and paper.

I offer them with hands of fire, asking if you
can decipher the image in ash.

Calendar

Cardinal

My wife likes to say we're a bundle of contradictions. She's up early, I'm up late. She's an A, I'm O. She believes in God but not eternal life, I pray for the opposite. So it happens that, through a combination of will and circumstance, I come to be standing on the patio with my clippers one July afternoon, considering an asymmetry of hostas and dwarf Alberta spruce and hearing in them the question that only plants can ask, having no consciousness—a tool manifesting first as cilia, then fins, then feet, and finally a CPU to gather it all. So programmed, the awareness that walks puzzles at itself, just as an obsessive-compulsive worries a mole, twists a handle—or a red bird beats at a window, trying to get at itself.

Bike Ride in Central Park

It starts with the sparrow hanging from the feeder
by one foot, feathers ruffled from a fight
with a jay, or simply from the struggle

to free himself, but in any case, pretty dead,
and looking to all the backyards like
the saddest sight we might see all week—

unless you were the neighbor whose sister
had just died from cancer, or the man whose father
had suffered a stroke and shat the bed.

Then the death of a single, mite-ridden sparrow
might not seem like such a big deal.
But it hijacked my thought during mid-morning

yoga, looking out the picture window
on coneflowers and obedient plant praising sky
with all their strength, black-eyed Susans

gossiping in busy groups, the coreopsis dead-
headed and aching for another try.
My mind wandered to the thought

that most often disturbs my thought:
I don't usually wake up with joy in my heart,
praising the day, glad to be alive, recalling Leah's

pleasure at Elizabeth Gilbert's instruction
to participate relentlessly
in the manifestation of your blessings.

I followed the tone of my life back and back:
pretty much A-minor all the way,
with a few variations into G.

Still, there's a certain tenderness in me
(I believe) in my desire to rid the lawn naturally
of a nest of bumblebees that sends out

messengers of intense sensation
every time I mow above their earthly home.
Two nights now I've run the hose

above their burrow, trying to persuade them
to the woodsier parts of what we call
our property to continue their pastoral visitations.

To be seen and not felt—which, I'm afraid,
might be corollary to the way I encourage
my wife of twenty-two years to unload

her griefs in order to unload her soul,
but preferably in certain time-allotted slots.
And so her joys. The spontaneous eruptions

make me feel (if you want to know the truth)
what I really feel. And though I'd love nothing
better than to unbuckle the armor that keeps

my heart from heaving whole into my mouth
(with joy, with grief— two sides of one coin),
that's still to some extent an abstracted desire.

Mostly, I don't want to suffer. Which makes me
suffer more: the warding-off, the holding
at bay while the whole ocean swells and waits

for me to plunge. As when last Sunday my stepson,
his partner, her toddler, and I rented bikes
to ride the Central Park Loop. It was given

to me to be the bearer of that three-year-old life,
strapped to the back of my bike in a child-seat
curved like the cradle of the moon.

I felt the trust and something-else
of that curious aliveness belted behind me.
I felt like the grandfather I'd never be.

I've known since I was nine I'd never father
children of my own. The earth had plenty
of people consuming and wasting,

pillaging, raping. She was groaning from the weight.
It was 1968, the year of *The Population Bomb,* of Tet,
of Nixon's election. I decided to make

some other contribution. So I helped raise Leah's son.
It's not that I'm against kindling the flame of life—
look at my garden, the tomatoes swelling

with converted sunshine and dirt.
And now my stepson helps raise someone
who will be his stepson, too. But my heart—

I was speaking about my heart, and the way
it fears to open. Because one morning I see
a bird hanging dead from the feeder that we use

to lure little wild lives to our kitchen window.
Because I try to urge some bees—tenders
of bright beauty and pain—away from my lawn,

but I *will* annihilate them, if it comes to that.
Still, I need to remember how at the end
of the ride, after speeding down hills for the thrill

of thrilling the child, dodging other bikes
and skaters and walkers and fine white horses
drawing fancy white carriages—there, in the crowd

by the gate that signaled the end of the park
and a return to streets and straight lines,
I got off and walked beside the bike because

that's what the sign said to do, and taking
one hand from the handle to my turn my hat
back around the whole bike slid sideways

in sand on the sidewalk, and down went
precious baby. Three men from Honduras
rushed to the rescue, as protective of that little life

as Rafael had been of his mid-ride ice cream.
The men uprighted the bike, laughing,
the boy still belted into his pod.

I thanked them, then mounted and wobbled
to a start. Raf sat in silence as we rode
toward the bike shop, until, at a crosswalk,

he announced, "Bike fall down." Which was
to say, though he was only three, "Life goes on.
Don't worry so much about it."

Then I handed him off to his mother,
who feathered him with little kisses.
And then it was time for lunch.

All the Things I Should Have Done

Pruned the forsythia.
Dug out the crabgrass before it spread to the neighbors' yards.
Studied up on crow so I could understand what they keep trying
    to tell me from the trees.
Made the coffee last longer.
Made the bed sooner.

All the things I rightfully regret—
I could go on and on.
The list would quickly bore you.

I should have found the source of fungus flies and bathed them in
    ammonia.
Should have stayed in bed an hour longer so I could find out how
    that dream ends.
Should have forgiven the jackhammers up the street, knowing
    someday I'll hire my own.

I'm trying hard to avoid the obvious, the sentimental.
Anything to do with mom or dad, with my sister's adopted baby,
    my brother's adopted baby, the issues with my wife simmering
    two days past the limit.

I shouldn't have sent that email, but I was tired of editing.
Should have avoided the highway, when what I wanted was a tree-
    lined street, but I was conflicted about the intersections.
Should have thanked the cashier from my authentic heart, instead
    of adding another layer of whitewash to the day.
Should have exercised more.

I shouldn't have eaten more than I really needed, heedless of starving
    children.
Shouldn't have drunk so much. Of anything. Except wine, maybe.
    One glass. Fully.
Should have interrogated my hunger and thirst.

I'm well aware of all the advice about the *shoulds* and the *shouldn'ts:*
"Don't *should* on yourself," the Brooklyn guru reminded us,
though in private he gnaws on his mother's curses.
Who made no distinction between guilt and shame, though he should
have.

Why didn't I open my heart even to him, since I couldn't to the
President?
Why didn't I start smaller, since I couldn't save the whole world?
Why didn't I pull those weeds by hand, instead of the aerosol shortcut
that drifted onto the hosta, and though it didn't kill them, uglied
their edges?
Why did I clap so loudly at that chipmunk scolding from the pine
branch, each of us more than a little defensive?

I should have simply stepped into her shoes, instead of fearing mine
would be ruined.
I should have simply told the truth.

Variations on a Theme in Red and Night

I need a car to drive to the woods
where I can walk away from drivers and cars

like I need the ticking of the clock to break
into a symphony of dactyls and iambs.

I need porpoises to surface into
who they really are and dive down

into who they really are.
I need to get up from the chair

where I am pinioned by words
and open the book with wings

to learn how to open my breast
wide enough to sail.

———

The simple thing is the most beautiful thing
I saw yesterday, leaning in on a single aster,

and when I looked closer at its fifty petals
and the three hundred leaves of its sunny face

that would, in a few days, give themselves over
to seed and make a thousand new flowers,

the universe opened up to me
its great dark secret, its precipitate emptiness,

littered with stars and planets
and the dust of attraction.

———

The future teases with figures of the past
so the story of my life I'm inventing

unfolds in reverse,
revising itself before it is made.

———

I pull the string that works the curtains,
which fall like underskirts.

I look into the soup that has simmered
for an afternoon: my mother scolds,

then reaches for my hand, then disappears
into its inscrutable ingredients.

———

Three squirrels dillydally in the yard,
collecting, forgetting, fighting, twisting

their silly helixes, apparently witless
but nevertheless nervous about winter's onset.

———

I know we're doomed, but come here and hold me
until my shoulders ache from letting go and I fall

into the sleep that feels like waking, or its opposite,
dreaming of snakeskins and lilies.

———

The sun almost speaks to me
from its treehouse in the maple,

sending down dots and dashes
in yellow and red. Without syntax

I am deaf. I spin, my arms like blades
gathering the emptiness.

Want

All I've ever wanted
is to want. I open my mouth
and instead of answers
want comes out. I want
more electricity and more
capital. I want the clay
and imagery of my life
to stand up and dance
with me, mirroring
my movements
one-for-one.
That would be
answer enough.
Instead, what I get
is half-made men
and women going
about their business
of wanting, too. I half-
dance for them in turn.
We form a cockeyed
web turning about
an imagined center.
It's here, it's here, no
over here. If someone
could trace its manic
path they might think
they'd discovered a kind
of map, an understanding,
like the fireflies' curlicues
spelling out something
other than tireless ache.

Calendar

Once, before there was counting—
but there was always counting—

if not the divide of six days
and a Sabbath, then the idle

and desperate annular scrawling
on cave walls that became

religion and agriculture
all at once.

That slow kind of cutting—
not this division of the living room

into rectangles and rounds
and the day labor to pay for it all.

Once, we listened to a running below rocks
instead of the dishwasher—

its constant hum reminding us
not so much of nothing

as of ticking and the urge
we've still not named.

Wind

And now a ticking behind me, the whirr or whine of some small spinning insect or filament or maybe the distant hum of a great engine pulling its vast array of coal and chemicals to be turned into this light I write by, this ink. Like it, like these, the mind lays down its scripted melodies, flashes that soon enough vanish, or rather reform into— what? A breeze of pulses that feeds a tree that feeds an ant or bird that serves some other form. And on, anon. Maybe sleep is what I need. Some silent healer, working behind the scenes. But there is no silence, no rest, and everything is visible, though we cannot see.

So

So

Ten miles below my mother's navel, I turned
in the green light. A thoughtless amphibian
unknowing of a decade of iron just passing
and a decade of fire just coming in.

In the course of my life the world would go
to its hell. Tornadoes rip Wall Street, the seawall
too low to keep the Atlantic from Broadway.

This is the compact the world has made
with its maker: an assurance that the thing
comes unmade on a regular basis, sand
recalling rock, rock in turn recalling plants

and the horrible pressure. Ammoniac oceans
and the mad swirl of atoms spewed in a moment
or two after the original idea. In the green light

I knew, but didn't let on, that destruction
is necessary, and a waste. That is, tragic,
in the sense that there may be an order to things.
A rightness that cuts. The history of terror

and transformation, of happiness and loss.
These are what make the green light
shift to sere, as if to say: "Behold."

And for it to be so. With a rending.

Documentary

That was the year El Niño made us doubt if
winter would come at all. But winter would come.

That was the century we took note
of how long dinosaurs roamed and how long
the blink of an eye really was. Blink.

Down in the trenches we fought
about usage versus syntax, about how far
the neighborhood of love really extended,

about the proper arrangement of furniture
and voting districts and other bulwarks
against the sureties of cancer and angina.

Meanwhile, over our heads, clouds raced
and birds flew confused along the old flyways.

Meanwhile, under our feet, continents
floated and crashed. High tides loaded
with VOCs threatened the big towns,

and we continued the old dance
to which we gave different names,
still hiding from knowing quite why.

Down in the deepest hole we ever made,
we sought silence and an answer,
the data always corrupted by our longing.

We threw our arms wide to the universe
aching for embrace. Angry, alone, and afraid,

we uncorked another bottle against the steel
of a vessel loaded with warheads
we named after our mothers.

With or Without Purpose

To believe you will go to heaven
and lie down with seventy-two virgins
for shooting a rabbi during prayer,
you have to ignore a lot of parts
of the book that gives one of the names
of God as Al-Ghafoor, Most Forgiving.

Today it's partly sunny here, which means
partly cloudy, too. Last night's rain
has melted half of last week's snow.
Last night we laughed at the party
around the table loaded with princely
snacks and cocktails, trying to keep
our human weaknesses belted in.

Compared to the reign of dinosaurs,
the small mammalian accident
that goes on two feet and kills
for abstract reasons has lasted about
an hour of the day called animal life,
and that day less than a second in the year
since light first cracked open the darkness.

Something in a friend's brain explodes,
and he enters the last sleep
without knowing or even a goodbye.
Another believes that the rocks themselves,
still cooling after their unbelievably distant birth,
are destined to discover that unique note
they will sing at the final banquet.

To believe you will go to heaven
and watch movies all day and that the popcorn
will be free and the roof will not leak

is not so incredible. In the basement of the
white clapboard house on the left, children
rehearse a play they just wrote; and in
the basement of the white clapboard house
on the right, horrible atrocities.

Solve for x

Here's what I know so far:
Chicken have feet.

Trees have leaves,
and Trump has Pence.

Mercy has no limit,
but forgiveness is hard to get,

as oceans have fish, and fish
gave the world reptiles

and all the other things that crawl
or walk, e.g., chickens.

Oceans have mammals, and once
a few decided life was better back there—

colder and darker, yes, but also
buoyant and unspeakably moist.

And charity has no limit,
but love is hard to come by,

as the movies now have sound,
but once they went 3D they reached

a certain limit: People got bored
and stopped supporting parks.

Everyone stayed inside,
eyes glued to possibility,

the economy a factor, but only
one: the solution always x.

And friends have enemies, but,
really, few friends,

as night follows day, but we
know which is master.

As, at the end of the day,
it's hard to decide which

I like better: closing my eyes
or waking up.

Thursday

Chipmunks dig tunnels in the flower beds
and then go to work on the foundation,

so I set rat traps for them baited with peanut butter.
Last Sunday I came out with my coffee to find

a squirrel had set one off; it lay curled
beside the brooms in the patio corner,

looking at me as if to say, when I touched him
with the shovel, "Fuck off and leave me alone."

I laid him on the other side of the flower box
that Leah had filled with begonias, below

her son's birdhouse, which last Friday a raccoon ravaged,
paw prints and feathers his unashamed signature.

Monday the squirrel was gone, only mushrooms
where he'd lain. Today, one that might be him

hobbles about, scrabbling for seeds the sparrows
and titmice have dropped from the feeder.

Nothing that's alive wants to be anything else.

October Prayer

If a grey sky can be indicative
of a life lived in the long echo
of the snap of umbilical cord

and a farewell to the self of pure love
floating in a green light near the origins
of particle and wave,

then let leaves high in the maple
turning to their first autumn orange
be messengers of messengers

from the tallest, most foreign
angels that death is waiting
for your next accident

and, no matter how cautious
you are, you will only ever
catch one glimpse.

Let the call of crow bobbing
in the pines be the ungainly ugliness
in your life that you must accept,

and let its digging in the yard for grubs
be your digging—acrid food
of your often-rehearsed regrets.

Crow gives way to silence
in which you hear
another kind of stirring.

Perhaps skies stretching,
preparing rain, watering
the suffering earth.

Looking Out

Look how this morning
the light returns to the backyard
and fields behind.

Night is a memory
and in place of an absence
that gives it form
is a color we call black.

And look how on the lawn
the white is gone

leaving green circles
like islands

or planets scattered
and forming in the mind
constellations of a kind

and others massed
whole galaxies or

as some call them
patches as if
the ground
were quilted with them

and how under its sheet
the yard merges with the sleeping
field and yellow stubble

or dun or brown or ochre.

The field becomes a hill
climbing—becomes trees
that reach up with purple fingers

or magenta or sumac

or black against a sky
where after three days
of solid rain and grey

clouds part—
touched with rose
from early sun

and behind those—
blue—finally—
after three days

and behind it something
larger that we compare

finally to night.

Night Walk

To Be

Other travelers have, in fact, returned
to tell about the land beyond the bounds,
but never in detail, no kind of story.

Only that a silence spreading like thunder,
the green light, and coming home waits
for us on this side, though we press and press

to get to the other. One day something
gives suddenly, and we fall flat, as it were,
upon our very faces: except that this one,

looking back, as if into a mirror,
is no longer so proud or puzzled.

Could Death

Could death be a small pond
at dusk, the sun just disappeared
below the hills, and the water
a memory of slate and summer green
and the hide-and-go-seek sun's still
beating heart? It would signify a paradise,
of sorts, if there were a boat with oars
and a cabin on the other side
with friends, a full plate and a glass,
and one more fire.

It could be the cold silence
of space, abstraction to the nth degree.

But not nothing we could not know.

Night Walk

So tonight for the first time I notice
the space of the removed organ

filled in, the memory of a doubtless pain
that was by its presence a kind of pleasure

fading. Before surgery, oblivion
hovered not like a threat, but more

like a bet, a prerequisite class quickly
filling up, and me near the front

of the line, still deciding. Now the future
resumes its extravagant promise,

and the present, like a breeze
carrying the scent of someone else's

dinner, drifts over. Not something
I can capture, I keep walking

the broken street, a stranger occasionally
at a window, looking out.

While Waiting for the Report

The laundry.
The ticking of the coffee pot.
The sun elbowing its way between the curtain
and the frame when the plan was to sleep in
and make up for so much lost sleep. And then,
once I was awake, the sun muffled by
storm clouds from the south, tamer
after all that destruction.

The desk calendar busied with shorthand
and numbers like small dams
against the slippage of time.
The "told-you-so" of the clock.

Her bras hanging from green wire
drying in the basement, each right cup
now imaged with a red "x" for "maybe."

The seethe of air pushing through the broken weather-
stripping of the basement door and the front door as well.
All winter they complained about the loss of heat
and wasted expense. Now their song is almost
hopeful, like a candidate's promise.

The cream that swirls in my coffee, like
those clouds, spinning into a new form.
And my hunger following, satisfied for a time
after cereal. But never disappearing. Or, but once.

Bare ganglia of trees dotted now
with iotas of hope. More than hope.
These surely will unfold into hand-sized green.
Diurnal contracts with what feeds us.
And the annual revocation.

Today's list: folding and tucking
into drawers. A trip to the hardware store
and thirty-minute chores. Washing up.
Putting into place. Clearing towards afternoon,
with a forty-percent chance of rain tomorrow.

Poem for Tony's Socks

You were on my mind all that winter week,
Tony. Monday a friend had asked me to suggest
a few of your poems for her Into to Lit course.
Tuesday I was rummaging in my closet for paper,
when your socks made their way across my palms.
For eight years I had been wanting to write
about those socks, pilled and ribbed, nearly used up,
and for the next three I tried, but struggled with the ending.
How do you write a proper poem about something
almost worthless that someone so dear has left behind?

You had shucked them in my run-down apartment
at the Fine Arts Center and danced the hot, rough
pavement beside me to the beach, where we sat
on the sand in the shade of a pier that led nowhere.
It was the summer after my father had died,
the summer my marriage seemed to be dying.
My wife faced the water and silently wrote,
while you listened and had no answer,
which turned out to be the best answer.

So your image has danced in my mind all these years,
Tony or, rather, it's glided supine, the way I fly
in dreams, or the way you first tutored me
another summer three years before,
disabled on the floor of someone else's office,
your allergies fully fueled by Southern woods
and beating you mercilessly into surrender.

I was touched that you'd teach me
through your pain, when all you wanted
was to tear out your traitorous sinuses.
This is not how some people see you,
big-hearted and vulnerable, but rather galling

as those overzealous histamines that pricked
your tender tissues—a reputation you've nurtured,
maybe, since allergies can make you insane,
or maybe because that's how cynics have learned
to protect their sensitive hearts—

an idea which that Thursday came home
to me, as I lay supine myself on the couch
after dinner and a little too much scotch,
reading your poems out loud with my wife,
the snow drifting loose from the trees.
Leah read the one about trains that makes her cry,
so I read the one about you repaying your mother,
holding her "in the uncomfortable air
between the wheelchair and the tub,
until she begged me like a child
to stop." Four or five times I had to stop, myself,
so I didn't dissolve into big shameful sobs,

though I don't think there's anything really wrong
with crying; but early on I learned my lesson well,
which is why I've spent the last forty years
trying to unlearn it. "Why," asked my wife,
"does that poem make you cry?" And when I finally
could speak, I guessed it had something to do with
the courage to see your defects in such honest light.

Which is also a theme I'd been hitting that week
with my juniors who were reading *The Great Gatsby.*
I spent a lot of time on Chapter Two, which sets it all up,
and Chapter Six, where Gatsby tells Nick
how he abandoned his ladder to the stars
only for a kiss. So after covering the valley of ashes
on Wednesday, I spent the final fifteen minutes
on the blurred photograph of Myrtle Wilson's mother
that "hovered like an ectoplasm on the wall,"
shot by Mr. McKee, the most minor of characters,

who claimed to be in "the artistic game,"
but who was careless enough not even to notice
the fleck of foam he'd left on his cheek after shaving.

"Isn't it the job of the artist to take
what we look at each day and allow us to see it
with new eyes?" I threw out to the air
in a rhetorical way to the circle of teens,
their own eyes glazed and at a low tide
of blood sugar before the buzzer for lunch,
their hunger for meaning obscured
by their hunger for whatever ambiguous
concoction the State of New York
had prepared in the Multi-Purpose Café.

True, a few of those eyes may have glinted
with a sort of recognition, and maybe that's why
they packed up more slowly and themselves
hovered, their bigger questions straining for focus
in the widening aperture between their hearts
and the fidgety abyss of their bellies—

which was the kind of clarity I'd been trying
to suggest was Fitzgerald's whole point,
or one of his whole points. Your way to it
was to dive deep into the unromantic reality
Fitzgerald made beautiful in his work,
if not in his life. The way Gatsby is left
"watching over nothing." The way Nick has to be told
by the racketeer Wolfsheim, "Let us learn to show
our friendship for a man when he is alive, and not
after he's dead." The way Nick is left standing
in the rain, watching over his own particular nothing.
The way you say in "Two Trains,"
"What grief it is to love some people like your own
blood, and then to see them simply disappear."

Like my Dad disappeared, a little more each year,
not just the years since he died, but the way
we diminished from each other when the differences
of age should have mattered least. We were so alike
and liked each other so much that my mother's father
had dubbed me "Little Benjy," after him.
My school friends envied our closeness, the big bear hugs
he gave me or anyone, the rumble deep in his chest
like a gong that dreamed us to Nirvana for a moment,
until we woke up, as from a dream, forgetting.
As in college I began my own forgetting,
and my love turned to shame, and his love of angels
and crystals grew to compulsion, choosing stock trades
or lovers on the advice of an amethyst pendulum
he hung around his neck. As though he didn't
even need a ladder like Gatsby's to reach
the unbounded stars that he longed for.

But despite his assurances that he'd live
past a hundred, grief made him grow smaller,
and he shrank into the warren of minutiae
his house had become. On my last visit, I opened
my laptop to show him pictures of my family
and scrolled a little too far. His eyes widened at a view
of his living room I'd shot from the stairs—
his recliner and TV like islands in the ocean
of paper and baubles he'd surrounded himself with,
threatening to drown him. "Oh, my," was all he said.
I didn't have the heart to ask if he was shocked
to finally see, as Nick Carraway puts it,
"through new eyes at things upon which
you have expended your own powers of adjustment."
Or if he simply saw my scorn and the threat
of betrayal if I offered this as evidence to my siblings.
He didn't say more, and I quickly closed the lid.

And that was the last time I saw him, except for the
three days the next summer, his surgery fouled
by ginkgo and ginseng and other blood-thinning
elixirs he'd taken for life everlasting, ending in sepsis
from an orderly's careless hands. For three days
he gulped beneath an oxygen mask, sealed
in a coma, waiting only for a nurse named Angél
to unplug the machine that forced life into his cells.
And then no more gasping. Too late
for me to forgive him, too late to be forgiven.

We carried his ashes to Sunken Meadow,
the beach where he loved to walk and swim,
where I had learned as a kid the prone glide
and the crawl. We spoke a few words in a circle.
Three times I tried to choke out the last lines
of "In Blackwater Woods" that Leah had chosen:
"to love what is mortal…and, when the time comes
to let it go, to let it go." Then my brother sprinkled
what remained into Long Island Sound.

I watched the ash dissipate, waited
for the unseeable remnant. The wind
did not come up. The little waves continued
their poor clockwork. Children down the beach
came closer, threatening the ghost in the water.
I thought, thought again, then threw away thought,
dove into that nimbus of ashes, hoping that
the hole I'd made in salt would never fill up.

So, Tony, one night after lying on the couch
reading your poems back and forth with Leah,
using your words to learn again how to talk
to each other, after years of silence in my closet,
your socks began to compose themselves into this,
patched out of pieces, like Mary Shelley's monster,

called into creation by a longing for completeness,
born the same year as your cancer, a synchronicity
I resist like I resisted my father's faith, from a fear
of being duped, of giving in to a wish for a life
that never ends, which is all I've ever wanted.

After two summers of writing, I thought the poem
was done and sent you a copy. You thanked me,
politely, and said you'd have more to say later.
Then I heard you were "circling the wagons."
I waited, not sure if I was inside or out,
but Meyer Wolfsheim's warning rang
clear in my mind, and I wrote you again.
"Yes, it's been rough two years," you wrote back,
"but the sky is falling for everyone, yes?"
And a few months later, "Not able to say much
right now—I'm in the thick of it."
Then silence, then the news you were gone.

I bought your last book, looking for a lasting
last message, and found it in your poem
for your father, and maybe all fathers:
"Tell him no matter how far off you are,
you are always living in his country;
tell him you yourself are an envelope
mailed from his address,
posted with a stamp that has his face on it."

Too late to thank you for that kind of forgiveness,
I'm holding on to your socks, Tony,
worn at the heels, washed to white thinness,
lodged in my closet beside the old notebooks.

January 10, 2015—December 31, 2019

The Questions

The Questions

Come to think of it, I like the questions better
than the answers. A question brings an opening,
as after a week of cloudy days a patch of blue

fresh in the east. Why does one squirrel
chase another in arabesques around the hostas
and yellow cypress? Is it a territorial dispute?

A courtship contest? Maybe they're just playing.
Why arabesques? How do the chipmunks know
winter is coming, scurrying here and there,

their cheeks puffed like Santa's great bag? How
do they remember where they hid their cache,
when day after day they return to the rat traps

set for them, licking off the peanut butter
and foiling the hammer most days but one?
Where do their souls go after I drop

their pretty bodies onto the leaf pile?
Do they even have souls? Do we?
Some questions open out like that,

hazy and distant, but all the same
unshakeable, the kind that give rise to religion
and government and all that hegemony. What

is a man? What is the proper role of a husband,
of a wife? When is the best time to fish or cut bait?
Leaning back in a green plastic lawn chair

in the hazy August night, waiting for remnants
of comets to trace a sky already glowing
with the amber of streetlight pollution,

these are the things I wonder. The mind
wants to clamp down and give answers. It's not
that I deny science. The best science, you know,

only offers answers that beget bigger questions:
If the universe is expanding, what's it expanding *into*?
If God is dead, to what do we keep praying? If the law

of tooth and claw is how we got here, why do we love
surrender just a little more than good sex?
Even the easy questions have uncertain answers.

What time will you be home? What *should* I have
gotten you for the twenty-fifth annular return
of our first and final betrothal? Do I really

remind you of your father? Yes or no
answers are the worst, in a way, because
under each syllable lies a story that might never

be told, and meanwhile off we go in our wobbly,
separate orbits, approaching perihelion, but still
missing, the most important messages

blown aside by the breezes of our passing.
What do you see when you look in the greens
of my eyes? How have we come all this way

and still remained strangers? Maybe I can help you
with that? Maybe you could hold this for me?

Maybe It Will Rain Today

And maybe it will snow.

And maybe when the postman
works on Sunday he will
momentarily lower
the tracking wand
and stand at the door
and tell us about his children
and listen to us brag about our grandkids.

And maybe the grass will give way
to forest and we will live
among the trees
listening to thrushes
in the overstory
their talk echoing
off trunks of oaks
without applying to us.

And maybe the universe will finally
arrange its mad swirl into a
harmonic convergence
and I will not judge
my neighbor for his love
of the President and automatic weapons
but understand his fear
and link arms, break bread, exhale.

And then again maybe
my own pocked heart
will heal over, the scars
soften and disappear and love
erase all boundaries.

Meanwhile a few white flakes
begin to fall, maybe
for a kind of answer
to a question not asked.

May Resolution

What if, instead of this slow dying,
we took one step more than improve
our diets and other resolutions?

Rearranged the furniture, or replaced
it entirely? The books and old clothes,
broken tools and picture frames, too,

built a bonfire in the backyard
and piled it high with these
and other shadowed doubts.

Now the new sofa we sit on, though
we might have chosen a darker color
or a lighter one, becomes an absolute,

a cradle of unending promise.
Where the old carpet lay like a field
of cinnamon and nails, now gleams

the glassy surface of still waters
we delight to walk on (bare feet only,
please, anything else brings a sinking).

Instead of books, we read
the world and its many pages,
turning like pear from linen

to green to bare and back again.
We delight to take three steps forward
and two back, freeing in the dance

the old darkness, stale like morning
breath, sashaying in the momentary
awakening before the next darkness,

like slicing into a fat lemon,
the hour suddenly burning with scent,
the only light we can know.

Prayer

for Tony

If you could fly, after they've stowed you
safe in earth or lit you like Friday

night's bonfire, would you fly to me
and, in your generous way, rain down

one drop of wisdom before you lift
finally into unfathomable lawlessness?

A pinch of understanding, a hunch, at least.
I don't ask for prognostication, that curse. Who

wants to know what you now know—
the time and circumstances of your end?

And as for the dissolution back into
the great dark ocean, who can grasp

that raveling? That every day might be
our last is fact enough. What I ask

is a clearer view. To heed the junco
lit like slate that scours the new-sprung ground

as long as she will stay. To gain the final stage
of our forgiveness, slough off the past,

and love again as children. That.
The evening looms with threat and terror,

which I try to douse with fire in a cup.
Spread your wings and cover me, dear friend.

I will inhale your ash like benediction.
Be my blood.

April, Month of My Birth

The garden edging has been moving
all winter towards its natural state of falling.

Now wild onion, sister of the lily, moves in
among the beds to reassert the edict.

The lawn's skin shows in patches
where snow lay heavy, thawed, froze again

like my own, where marks of birth
have been iced and slowly slough off.

In a blink, all disappears
and is replaced again.

I came here like a messenger.

What will I carry home?

Where I Came From

Emergence

Slate Cove, Lake Skaneateles

It's the hour
      when everyone's

feet are blazing

    with October woods
      drowned limestone

      grandmother's cookstove
        a wet dog on the back porch

    strangers with messages
      pinned inside their sleeves

We're walking
    out of dark silences
and lost thought

      like water
        slapping a boat—

    behind us always

      no matter how many
        times we turn our heads

Beyond us in the dark

    things are stirring

as if waking

Even in the afternoons
    running from work
        to market to home

a lingering scent
    like lemon

        a quick view

through warped glass
    at tangled blues

    and reds
        still swaying

as if they were trees

      goodbyes

  or greetings

Work

I sweep the back porch of maple keys
and oak flowers from last week's storm,

bring out the rocker, my tools:
lapdesk, notebook, pen, coffee, apple.

A chipmunk winds up his chipping warning
like a crazed mason working a wetted stone.

The sparrow on the spruce bough gurgles her question,
unsure how to get the moth in her beak to the birdhouse

near me where her chicks gawk and chitter.
One of the flagstones is crumbling to dust,

and later I'll look into why, and later repair it.
Later weed the garden, mow the incessant lawn,

negotiate paths between love and ruin
that separate the kitchen and bedroom.

Make lists. But for now there's this work,
these small strokes, maybe nothing more

than compost for tomorrow's garden.
Everything I see is made of small efforts,

piled like pebbles to divert some current
this way or that. It narrows and roars, flattens,

makes a fan from which slender green things
grow. A web of small lives, digging, leaping,

soaring. Gathering twigs and making nests
shaped like a world, for the work to continue.

Cure for Thought

Put a new load of clothes in the washer
as though they were thoughts.

Hang wet laundry, as though it were thoughts.

Shuck dried green beans that dried
on the old door screen in the joists for two weeks.
Bring to a boil and let soak one hour.

Walk to the store in rain for celery.

Count trees with leaves still wholly green.
Smell the tang of those fallen ones like recurrent thoughts
returning to earth for another round.

View ghosts in shop windows
as if they were someone else's.

Make small talk with the cashier
as if she were your grandmother as a young girl,
lip-ring and iPhone of no consequence.

Return the way you came,
viewing the same trees and sky from the other side.

Chop vegetables. Rinse beans. Throw all
with ham hock into a large pot. Cook until tender.

Ladle into pint jars. Process in a pressure canner
at 11 pounds for one hour.

Let cool.

Set in a dark place.
Listen.

Why We Danced

We danced because there was nothing else we could do. The bottom had fallen out of everything, a dog barking in the sweltering dark barring the way to a house we weren't sure was ours. Inside, we heard the sound of something being beaten—a child, a man. Or maybe they were laughing. Maybe they were making love. Maybe it was a drum.

It was the darkness that got in the way because there was red in it. And the heat, too, because inside were moments of cool, spaced by friction, as if by design, though one I did not understand. It slowed me.

So we danced. We found each other in the dark that was not completely dark, through grunts and cries and kisses that became something like a language. A bridge.

Once in a while, the dog stopped barking, maybe because it heard something of itself in our calls. And the house grew quiet for an hour, so we danced.

Cradle

No matter how I try to dodge it or what accidents
of fate impede, the green light persists
in dogging me like, well, a dog, or a light

that's green, sifting in through windows after hours,
in my dreams, or every evening when I sit
on the back porch, or every morning, same.

As today, slyly circulating around the edges,
suggesting its presence like a quiet fever,
until someone says a word, the right one

or wrong, and a lungful of air swells, fanning
anger's flame, coals of fear below, great puffs
of black smoke showing something is cooking.

Then, sure enough, crass confessions burst
like bombs—*I hate you as much as I love you!
Loving you is like pouring water on a rock!*

The netted world flashes whole. Into one
crack the weird light creeps—green
from a world outside time, and not

to be recovered. Molten hues
of red and yellow, bathing within
some fragile, sweet pink thing.

Bird Time

I'm off the clock now,
on garden time, book time,
bird time, almost.

I know what day it is: June 30.

And the meaning of the increase
of traffic over where the sun falls
halfway through its tilt.

How I didn't cry yesterday
when I was with you,
though maybe I should have.

How I long for more friends
and better ones.

Still, the birds come back, mixing
with the poison of the evening commute
on the other side of the spruces.

Shadows of light after rain,
unequaled for their capacity to make me feel

as I felt when I was four
about this time of day.

Someone was burning his fields.

Over the world, and filling it, and me,
a scent. A quality
of afternoon.

An hour.

When God Visits Me

When God visits me He appears at first as a smell
of citrus in my wife's hair

and the next morning as a certain oppressive
yet beautiful humidity after the 3 a.m. thunderstorm.

The day after that, I'm lying on the couch
when He emerges from my belly button,

reminding me of the old days
when I swam in the green light beneath my mother's navel

and anticipated life like a birthday
instead of a sentence that grows more predictable as it nears its
    conclusion.

God waves all that aside with a gesture
of layered clouds viewed from a hammock

at 8 p.m. on a night in June.
"There, there," He coos, as His hand moves in slow circles

over that particular place on my back
that lets me know I am loved.

Starry Nights

Yes, there are other animals
that mate for life—
but that doesn't mean they get
to sit on the sidewalk outside

Starry Nights on July 28
just after a long drought—
you drinking ginger green tea,
I a latte in a heavy white mug.

The air is soft after rain,
the half-moon floating lazy
and sort of blue and amber
above the high haze.

A trio is playing,
and because the guitarist
sings like Chet Baker
the night gets sweeter
than nutmeg cake.

Diaphragm

The house finch sipping at the birdbath
darts a look at me, then at the water

saying, *Just breathe.* Flits off,
a blur of russet not intended

for my interpretation. A squirrel
on the spruce branch works the husk

of a black walnut, his belly and spine
ringing *Winter,* though August isn't

finished yet. *Just breathe,* the backyard says
again in silent bells, unaware of anything

like tragedy. A sparrow takes a turn at water.
The squirrel, nearly finished gnawing,

cascades through a cedar shrub,
hurrying to bury his cache

until another comes to spy, as if
either will remember come January.

And here I am, reporting it all
from my back porch, diaphragm

weary from restraint. Memory nags,
an incessant mosquito at one ear,

while the future remonstrates, alternately
wagging and curling one long finger.

When I finally step aside
and let this body be what it is, noticing—

the pool of time empties,
fills. Traffic on the highway swells,

diminishes. The redbud prepares its pods.
A breeze lifts the spruce boughs.

Where I Came From

no one asked for help
        or a gentle word
    or a reassuring pat
on the arm—

those were things
            given
        almost
every hour

between moving
    the chopped
            vegetables
    from the counter
to the pan

when getting
        into or out of
a vehicle

        whenever
    any heavy lifting
needed doing

Where I came from
    the seas
        were always dark
and whispering

their secrets
    in six or seven languages
        we'd never heard
    before

but understood because
    water
        was our mother
    and through her
the thread of fire

from the first
    sun's
        ignition
    ran straight
as an arrow

Here
    we make myths
    to try to explain
why we draw
    the cloak over—

an unexplainable act
    like the origin
of atoms

Here
    we have only history
no real causes

just this
    and then this—

In that way
    it's just
like home

It waits
    for us
        just this side

of trying so hard

to pretend
   we're not
pretending

Where I come from
   it's just this breath—
      this kiss—

then this—

Notes

The epigraph is from *Kabir: Ecstatic Poems,* translated by Robert Bly, published by Beacon Press (2011).

Quotations in "Poem for Tony's Socks" are from *The Great Gatsby* by F. Scott Fitzgerald, published by Charles Scribner's Sons (1925), and Tony Hoagland's works in the following order of appearance: "Lucky" in *Donkey Gospel* (1998), "Two Trains" in *What Narcissism Means to Me* (2003), and "Rain-Father" in *Priest Turned Therapist Treats Fear of God* (2018)—all published by Graywolf Press. "In Blackwater Woods" is by Mary Oliver, from *American Primitive,* published by Little, Brown (1983).

Acknowledgments

Thanks to the editors and staff of the following publications in which these poems first appeared, some in slightly different form:

Barrow Street: "October Prayer," "Want"
Before After/Godwink (bagliterary.com): "Cradle"
Borderlands: Texas Poetry Review: "Solve for x," "While Waiting for the Report"
Cimarron Review: "Delivery," "Cure for Thought"
Dime Show Review (dimeshowreview.com): "Brief History"
DMQ Review (dmqreview.com): "Work"
Eunoia (eunoiareview.wordpress.com): "Night Walk," "To Be"
Lake Effect (Penn State): "The Questions"
Rust+Moth (rustandmoth.com): "Documentary"
Slush Pile Magazine (slushpilemag.com): "Calendar"

"After Easter" (entitled "Christmas Eve,") and "Looking Out" first appeared in *Another and Another: An Anthology from the Grind Daily Writing Series,* Matthew Olzman and Ross White, eds. Durham, NC: Bull City Press (2012).

Thanks to the following for their encouragement and friendship:
—Members of the Warren Wilson MFA community: Martha Rhodes, whose comments early on steered me towards stronger writing. Online workshoppers MaryLou Buschi Daniels, Karen Fein, Megan Gillespie, and Debra Gitterman. And Dinah Berland, Wendell Hawken, Annie Kim, and Rosalynde VasDias for their generous manuscript feedback.
—Sarah Freligh, for a friendly and firm manuscript review.
—My current writing group for close reading and camaraderie: Charlie and Danielle Coté, David Forman, and Alicia Hoffman.
—Lesley Williamson and the Saltonstall Foundation for a place to write and gaze out the window.
—Ross White, for his shepherding of the Grind Daily Writing Series. At least a third of these poems were written under that happy pressure.
—Diane Kistner, for her thoughtful editing and her love of poetry.

Gratitude and love to Leah and Brian, who know me best and help me understand.

About FutureCycle Press

FutureCycle Press is dedicated to publishing lasting English-language poetry in both print-on-demand and Kindle formats. Founded in 2007 by long-time independent editor/publishers and partners Diane Kistner and Robert S. King, the press incorporated as a nonprofit in 2012. A number of our editors are distinguished poets and writers in their own right, and we have been actively involved in the small press movement going back to the early seventies.

We award the FutureCycle Poetry Book Prize and honorarium annually for the best full-length volume of poetry we published that year. Introduced in 2013, proceeds from our Good Works projects are donated to charity. Our Selected Poems series highlights contemporary poets with a substantial body of work to their credit; with this series we strive to resurrect work that has had limited distribution and is now out of print.

We are dedicated to giving all of the authors we publish the care their work deserves, offering a catalog of the most diverse and distinguished work possible, and paying forward any earnings to fund more great books. All of our books are kept "alive" and available unless and until an author requests a title be taken out of print.

We've learned a few things about independent publishing over the years. We've also evolved a unique and resilient publishing model that allows us to focus mainly on vetting and preserving for posterity poetry collections of exceptional quality without being overwhelmed with bookkeeping and mailing, fundraising activities, or taxing editorial and production "bubbles." To find out more about what we are doing, come see us at www.futurecycle.org.

The FutureCycle Poetry Book Prize

All full-length volumes of poetry published by FutureCycle Press in a given calendar year are considered for the annual FutureCycle Poetry Book Prize. This allows us to consider each submission on its own merits, outside of the context of a traditional contest. Too, the judges see the finished book, which will have benefitted from the beautiful book design and strong editorial gloss we are famous for.

The book ranked the best in judging is announced as the prize-winner in the subsequent year. There is no fixed monetary award; instead, the winning poet receives an honorarium of 20% of the total net royalties from all poetry books and chapbooks the press sold online in the year the winning book was published. The winner is also accorded the honor of being on the panel of judges for the next year's competition; all judges receive copies of all contending books to keep for their personal library.

www.ingramcontent.com/pod-product-compliance
Lightning Source LLC
Chambersburg PA
CBHW070041110426
42741CB00036B/3114